# Black Sugar

*By the same author*

*Fiction*

Inhabiting Shadows
Isidore
Delirium

*Non-Fiction*

Madness – The Price of Poetry
Lipstick, Sex and Poetry (autobiography)

*Poetry*

Nineties

Jeremy Reed

# *Black Sugar*

## *Trisexual Poems*

*With drawings by* Jean Cocteau

Peter Owen
*London & Chester Springs PA*

PETER OWEN PUBLISHERS
73 Kenway Road London SW5 ORE
Peter Owen books are distributed in the USA by
Dufour Editions Inc. Chester Springs PA 19425–0449

First published in Great Britain 1992
© Jeremy Reed 1992

A catalogue entry for this book is available from
the British Library

ISBN 0 7206 0876 1 (pb)

Printed in Great Britain by Billings of Worcester

## Acknowledgements

Some of the poems in this collection first appeared as follows:

'Love' in *The European Gay Review*, Vols 8/9; 'Playing with Fire' and 'Purple Banana' in *The Literary Companion to Sex*, ed. Fiona Pitt-Kethley (Sinclair-Stevenson, 1992); 'Shoe Fetishist', 'Transsexual', 'Voyeur' and 'The Insatiable' in *Nineties* (Jonathan Cape, 1990); 'Feet on Shoulders' in *Sphinx 3*; and 'Jewels' in *Madness – The Price of Poetry* (Peter Owen, 1989). 'Shoe Fetishist' has also appeared in *The Literary Companion to Sex*.

# Preface

The erotic is always an incomplete history of the senses. Incomplete because we incessantly return to it, hoping that each new encounter will appease the impossible demands made by the imagination. In that respect, sex is like poetry: both carry an orgasmic thrill that is connected to arrival, discovery, the burn-up of nerve as we chase images across inner space. And it's the engagement of all the senses that the two should share in common, the sustained moment, the realization that we are most alive in the adrenalin rush that has us overtake ourselves.

Black Sugar is a girl who steals for sexual kicks. Jean Genet did likewise. I chose to write a poem about Lou Reed's song 'Kicks' because that's still another dimension. We are all a multiplicity of selves, and we may choose to live out our fictions or consign them to imaginative embodiment. The doing is dependent on whether we are willing to accommodate risk or pathologize it as a taboo.

It seems to me that any poetry worth its name should be involuntarily fuelled by a need to subvert convention. The surrealists incorporated the erotic into their artistic credo. Too often, English poetry confuses the sensual with smut, addresses the anatomical instead of the protean image that gender should assume.

When I began writing poetry as a schoolboy, I found my awareness of a bisexual orientation inseparable from poetic intention. Classification, categorization, reductionism, represented the dead world, one of limits rather than expansion. Neither poetry nor sex should be about acceptance; they should embrace exploration, a fluency that allows the individual to travel between parallel dimensions, taking in the multiple permutations of experience that duality affords. Maybe I misread English poetry, but I don't find in it the lyric voluptuousness that I do in Breton, Lorca, Éluard, Neruda, Genet, to name but a few of the poets who have celebrated the erotic as an extension of the imagination.

Most of my erotic poems explore fetishism, an attachment to obsessive detail. The man who hunts through hotel wardrobes to add a pair of shiny thigh-boots to his stash, could be me, but it isn't. I don't have to be in any of the poems any more than the photographer need intrude on his subject. Where I am is in direct sympathy with everything that creates new modes of sexual expression – the sci-fi poem in this book makes possible sex between a directed eye-beam and an aperture in the partner's navel.

Predictability breeds boredom. It is the latent, unrealized potential within the individual to consummate fantasies which seems important. Bipolar tendencies are often there as blips in the unconscious, impulses waiting to attune to a shift from lateral to bilateral thought.

My book about poetic commitment, *Lipstick, Sex and Poetry*, was also an evaluation of gender flexibility. How boring it must be for a man never to have made up nor to have experienced awakenings to the possibilities of being the opposite sex. Or one sex. What we see from men is the collective atrocity of warfare, and I come back to the psychic malfunction of mono-gender, the repression of the feminine within psyche which leads to masculine cloning. The poem 'Mutants' in this collection looks towards the extinction of the old order. Sexual stereotypes are like a film still that's got stuck, not for a rainy Sunday, but for an evolutive infinity.

I'm writing this at the end of an alley, a moment out of time, before the rain sets in. A notebook balanced on blue denim. Some of us live our lives waiting for metamorphosis, transformation, the body and the poem, the physical and the oneiric to unite in a quantum leap into the future. Sex without gravity, an indefinite suspension in which to imagine how or when it will ever happen. The old game for most people of trying to contact fantasies: the one spatial, the other temporal.

All things with style. The girl dressed in three green sequins and the man wearing a leather thong may have very different sexual directions, but a corresponding sympathy may lead who knows where. A geometry that becomes in time the memory of light in an angle of the room, the taste of vanilla on the tongue, a mutual understanding that switches on a billion unused brain cells. And above all a breaking down of patterns, the admission that everything is possible, that sex demands the sort of imagination associated with risk-taking poetry.

Jeremy Reed

# Contents

## Invocation

To all the blondes who have never turned their heads
in recognition of my androgynous beauty,
to all the black-haired girls walking in October sunlight
on the flame-coloured boulevards, hair blown away
on bridges above the leaf-whipped Seine,
to all the redheads who discover Kandinsky's
colour spirals energizing the still air.
To all the pink haired, green haired, violet haired
avant-garde liberators, for the men
who are women in disguise, transpeciated,
for all the android alternatives to the human,
love on a weird, parallel dimension.
To a beach at dawn, the red clouds like flamenco skirts,
for these words, the telescoping of metaphors
down afternoon alleys, and to green eyes
I dedicate my celebratory words,
this evocation of figurative possibilities.
The names Leanda, Liana, Rubella –
girls out on the beaches, men made up in bars,
to the obsessively modern image
looking a moment, a moment up at the stars.

## Scenes

Her purple bra. His purple hair.
They're photographed together and they're gay,
but back to back in leather thongs,
the sea behind them, they live out each day
as though it were their last, burn up on nerve

and conquest, individually.
A blue light draws a circle round the bay.
The stillness rings. It's late summer,
a patchy scrub of thistles rash the cliff,

each natural echo sounds like voice effects
happening out there in the haze.
The moment won't return. A wasp goes half
into the oval of an untabbed can

and then withdraws. He tells her of the man
he's never found – the one who'll walk
into his life one day, and how they'll know
each other, blue eyes brushing green.
Together, they'll be consumed by the sun;

love carries that intensity.
She can't find someone who will stay,
each time they leave her for a man.
It happened just before this holiday.

They're impatient for the night,
the waterfront bars, but now, hand in hand,
rush for the sea and kick up clouds of spray.

## Cocksucker Blues

### 1

Addressing head is the nearest we'll get
to realizing self-fellatio.
The taste is grenadine seeds, salmon roe.

### 2

A nervous orchestration. Oval lips.
Draw a red lipstick love-heart on the spot
where the tongue triggers. Scarlet, hot.

### 3

Condoms add colour from turquoise to black.
A two-tone body. It's a scorching trick
to nibble, wait, intermittently flick.

### 4

The rhythm's variable as reedy jazz.
For the one receiving it's a shampoo.
Honey can be added. The night is blue.

### 5

In sex, we wonder if the other one
has more or less pleasure, and when he shoots
a desert flower shows from volcanic roots.

### 6

A musical scale: slow, alerting all
the nerves to climax. It's a tornado
inside a drinking straw, starting to blow.

### Love

(after Jean Cocteau)

The twist of a knife is well worth a rose.
Let me kill you slowly,
expertly; your lover
changes you into a dead woman,
metamorphoses you into a beast, an inkpot,
until you shout it.

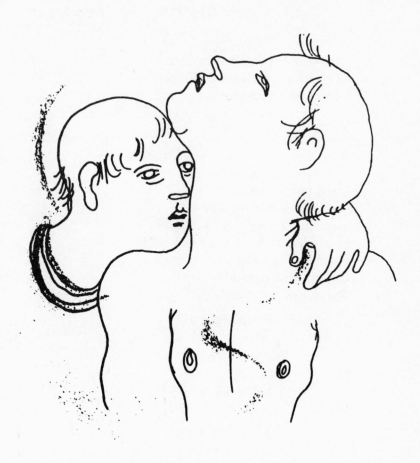

## *Playing with Fire*

You going down, contortionist,
to give me head with pink lipstick,
a black girl with red hair,
your face a locket. A green curtain drawn
on the afternoon rain.

Your vibrations drew the volcanic core
to a white tributary of fire
eased out as pearls.
Your drop-earrings shook
diamanté flashes, two waterfalls
responsive to your rhythmic tongue,
you lying in a black G-string,
conical breasts with nipples
like purple anemones.

I came, imagining seraglios
and all the positions we'd achieved,
the best one, your legs right over your head
in a three-quarters somersault,
I straddling as though suspended
taking off in a gymnast's vault.

## That Summer

A red lion entered your dreams.
Polio in the water, torrid dust
and a nightingale in eucalyptus.
You reading the Greek anthology
all these years and sea-storms later.

Who will hear us through?
What we've known, written and read
burns with a transparent flame.
Your intruder was sun-faced, red.

Night measured by throaty cries.
Toenails clawing a thin wall,
silken legs gone up so high.
Fierce love scales a ladder;
our redhead nocturnal visitor
burnt eye-holes in the night.

Villages lost to hills.
The sea was always in the sky,
my poem shone like mineral
coruscations split from rock.

We stayed a month. The lion wouldn't go.
Your see-through red nightie
was clear as a window,

ravaged by the lion's paw.

## Bees Stinging Words

Proust reads a scrip written out for morphine.
Sailor Blue angles a pen from his mouth

and leaves a broken red lipstick halo
on the maestro's conducting-stick.
Marcel knows time is money. He's on leave

and sails at three into a cobalt glyph.
The fried potatoes have a silver tit

clamped to their gold brought from the Ritz.
Sailor Blue talks about fellatio,

purple helmets flavoured with aniseed.
'I'd like to write my own biography,'

Marcel interjects. 'It's the only way
to falsify a fictional prism.
I'll call it *Drugs and Rats and Vetiver*.'

Celeste enters with his Le Gras powders;
the two disengage as on a film-flick,

an improvised 2,000 miles away.
Sailor Blue uses a Kleenex tissue

to take his make-up off. It is the night;
he slips outside into Albert's taxi,

and Marcel reads by a green-shaded light.

## *Love in the Afternoon*

The louvers on the Venetian blinds snap shut,
phasing out a beach-scene, a turquoise sea,
the beach-guards' improvised fibreglass hut,

fronting the cadenced surf, and by the quay
the black hotels coffined against the sky,
the burnt-sienna cliffs, a momentary

blue needle-frieze slatting into a dark
that's intimate. We've tented out the day,
our early explorations in a park

have brought us back to your hotel, not mine.
Your skirt is pinched down like a second skin,
a sort of shedding as you curve your spine,

your amber flush without strap-marks, your round
bottom visible through transparent net.
You bend down low. Your hair streams to the ground.

We're like a summer storm. Our bodies meet
in crazy hurricanes of fantasy
and what your hands don't supplement, your feet

find ways to do; we're a geometry
so oiled and intermeshed we've stretched ourselves
in one figure, a new anatomy,

a sinuous fluency, while outside
a heat-struck afternoon has swimmers run
in ones and twos to meet the rising tide.

## Hey

An end of it. Meeting like this.
It's an infraction on society
the things we do in public. You and I.
A red cherry trapped inside a crystal,
so the winter sunset seems,
an ideogram, a haiku, scarlet
efflorescence in a cone.

This way not that is what we know.
The risk, the meeting out of time,
your Paisley tie unmasted, vulnerable
to whatever the threat we undergo –
your wife, executive infrastructure.

We lose the hour; a dead moth hangs
its folded parachute in the window.

## Shoe Fetishist

His intimacy with hotels
clarifies the anatomy
of his circuit from the inside,
hall-porters, how to slip a key

from a receptionist, coerce
by adopting a strategy
of hinting at discrepancies
inherent in their policy

of desk-bribes, turning a blind eye
to the hooker using a suite
that's officially occupied.
His preoccupation's with feet,

the small, tapered, red toe-nailed foot
that silks into a stiletto,
wine-glass stemmed heels, the metal cap
exciting when he traces slow

abrasions with it on his skin.
Snakeskin, patent, black satin bows,
he adds them to his collection,
imagining silk-stockinged toes

forming a sensuous glove-fit
in the hard elongated point.
Smell, colour and tactility
shape in his mind a sculpted joint

between the arched sole and his sex,
an erotic intersection,
cupped in his hand intangibly
with variants of position.

His wardrobes are stashed with leather
exhibits; they're his solitary
communion with occupants
he's come to love vicariously;

and recalls the fired stimulus
of his great cache, his standing back
before thigh-high and knee-high boots,
almost uncrinkled in their black

austerity, the hotel dead,
mid-afternoon and how the air
was scented with them as he'd knelt
like one dropped to his knees in prayer.

## Feet on Shoulders

The season multiplies extravaganza;
such pink and crimson peonies heaped in a vase,

and the contained rose turbans, open silks
recalling a Fantin-Latour;

a blue vase on a black lacquered table.
Outside the air is musty with hawthorn,

a slowly assimilated aphrodisiac.
A phallocratic drive works through each tree.

I watch you undress tauntingly.
You balance on high heels in black panties,

a pearl necklace falling to your full breasts,
your body coppered by the sun.

You unclip earrings. The jasmine storms in.
Our window floods with a pink-indigo.

Legs arched, you place your feet on my shoulders,
two satin petals; and we flower as one.

## Black Sugar

Or call her the enigma. What she stole
or where she hid was a chiaroscuro
of worked-out guesses. She was singing soul

in a night-spot in hardly anything
under a focused spotlight when we met;
her hand loaded with sparkles, one blue ring

a diamond planet liquid with her wrist.
A girl thief who drove a pink truck,
her double actions emphasized the twist

that had her steal. When she was up on-stage
her character was unified; she lived
inside the song and not the spiral rage

that took her out to dark places alone,
or up to unlit apartments, her hands
wanting to do the things her mind had done,

anticipating this. There was a need
involved in her selection, a speed-flash
that thrilled her nerves, and a spontaneous greed

to loot and go. She got caught with the Ming
china, the owner came back, found her there,
and all that she could think to do was sing.

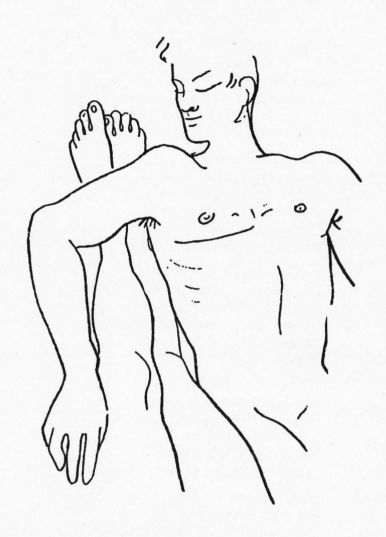

## Transsexual

A rickety table
in a dilapidated studio.
the poster of Garbo's
a reinvocation of *l'âge d'or*,
Hollywood Highs, a lipstick bow's
delineated indigo –

impossible to imitate
in poverty, the gelid room
with its opulent gilt mirror
from which a disapproving face
stares back in terror
where the stubble shows blue-lavender

through matt foundation.
Lipstick tubes, plastic razor,
a gold Bardot wig on its stand,
brushed and lacquered, it's the day
brings interminable ennui.
Night is a source of money –

selling out on a body,
arranging deals in alleyways,
always the fear, always the fear –
a miscalculated assignation,
informer or psychopath,
pusher burning for a stashed cache,

there's no retribution . . .
She reads a magazine at dusk
on fashion-tips. The blue turns black.
She checks her make-up, locks the door,
learns to balance on her heels.
There might be no coming back.

## Our Way

She dresses with her back to me
a vase and apple in congruity,
the black silk horizontal of her bra,
and how the curtain's a mauve waterfall
arriving soundlessly forms part of this
prelude to shifting dimension,

so she wears a red dress by the green sea
that's swollen, equinoctial,
starfish and bleached cuttlefish bones
raked by the seawall with boxes, battered fuel-drums;
a red light burns on the jetty.

Night, and she undresses, facing me.
I am the mirror in which she reflects
our interchangeability.
I wear her stockings on my hands as gloves,

we have our ways of sensuality,

and down below the big breakers
smoke whitely, crashingly into the cove.

## Mutants

We're really speeding and the days stand still –
they're open pages the wind turns over,
batiked by leaves. Red maples fire the hill

on which an S and M crucifixion
took place at night, the leather boys packing
beneath the trees. There's a new tension

to go beyond identity, move fast
towards a gender blueprinted in cells,
a species disinheriting the past

for unresolved extremes. Some have it now,
the mutant gene, the need for a body
to answer inner vision. It's so slow,

the old world's gradual extinction, I see
a girl with gold planets on dark glasses,
another star tattooed on her right knee;

her girl-friend's shaved head doesn't emulate
the male, it looks towards the arrival
of a sorority; and they are late.

Those of us who have known the psychic change
are looking out for signs. Did it begin
with the sixties, the implant of a strange

dress and drug culture which has picked up pace,
mutated inwardly from cult to cult
and now awaits the coming of its race?

## *Silk*

Its coolness imparts fire to touch.
It takes your line and celebrates
a curve, a contour, how a bottom rounds
into black and metallic green,
leaving the zip straight on the back.
The finger crackles on each tension-point.

You mould the dress so it excites,
vibrantly sheened petal that clings,
a volute-sheath.
It shivers as it warms to you
the way a slow wave smokes across a beach.

It's when it falls it frisks like autumn leaves;
a green silk in contact with black
beneath. It is a crown around your feet
you step out of as though a waterfall
was fire down your back.

## Pear in a Poem

A speckled nugget windfalled into grass,
a yellow, conish, sexual top
that's lost its spin, and the intrusive seam

is holed by wasps. Or the skin's leathery,
more like a lizard's colouring; and fit

two together, base touching base
and it's a union of satellites;
in earthly values, a green, spotted swede,
a yellow pepper with a woman's curves
and two stump tails. Stood up on a table
most wobble, lose their equilibrium.

A hand working itself between two breasts,
over the shoulder from behind
has a connection here, black satin cups
pushed down for freer play.

Pears haloed with mauve sea anemones.

Ripe fruit brings fullness to the mouth;
pear's more subdued than apple, less tangy,
and leaves equivocations in the bite.

When you zip up, your contoured skirt
makes your bottom a silk pear, it's so tight.

## Lisa Jane

She's on her haunches, and her lover tracks
a tongue-tipped silver furrow, finds the place
responsive to her coaxing, up and up
Lisa arches her bottom; Jane's gloved hands
stand out as black silk on each cheek,
while Lisa's face is hidden by a net,
her red mouth open as the pleasure builds,
her tongue seeming to roll a strawberry
as Jane registers each voluble shiver,
teases by stopping and then starts again,
this time with a rhythmic intensity
that rocks the bed, while it goes on and on
Lisa's convulsive pleading, she wants more
than any orgasm can satisfy.

Jane likes it differently, laid on her back,
talking out loud the fantasies
Lisa gratifies with finger and tongue.
It's slow, involving discourse, but the two
get high on it, provocative detours,
a circular motion of crotch-to-crotch
friction before Jane starts to lift,
demands the finger works with greater speed,
requests her black panties are taken down
by Lisa's kneading teeth. Later they lie
together, watch the pink-edged clouds
build oblong sculptures in the summer sky.

## *Transvestites*

We live the gender split as cross-overs
to an assumed identity. A game,
a risk, we're mostly volatile lovers

excited by transference; look, a twist
of silk around my neck, a lipstick gash,
a tinted foundation and I exist

as more alive, more consciously as me
than any other role I might adopt.
A public challenge? It's temerity

that's needed to confront the street; I try
to make it natural; red and black and white,
a pencil line drawn round each almond eye;

I am my own artistic creation,
I find the face I want to wear, select
my brushes for each primed situation

and meet it like that. It's unnatural
to be so recognizably the same;
most men will never know the ritual

that goes with making up. The risk is there,
also the joy of finding in strangers
a welcoming vindication, a stare

that's followed by a girl's smile, and we meet,
both brightly coloured, talking in the wind
that blows cherry blossoms across the street.

## Trans-elevation

She thinks curled up in leopardskin. It's right
his face and hands are silver and they sit
in a glass rectangle, one side shaded,
the others open to the street. The park's
subtropical; its rubber trees
point to occasional clouds, white and red
vaporous cubes. Her glass table's
a prism on which she places sea shells,
starfish – a beach by Yves Tanguy
contributes to the notion of mental space:

they talk about the deepening.
They've changed like the environment; no cars,
just helicopters and their sex
has part mutated. When she takes it in,
it's through the ear, fragile helix
evolved to an aperture.
Their future's a thing of the past
because they've gone beyond it and look back
at photographs of the old world. That's her
as someone else; that's him in drag
when it was necessary,
London, *circa* 1980, and both
taken by a friend beneath a plane tree.

## Drugs, Drag and Make-up

It's night, the shadow-self
encourages the gender split;
a break-off into opposites.
Julian has Caroline's fit

for a St Laurent party dress.
Where we go is a friend's house:
a roof-garden above the bay.
A shooting star burns a white peacock's tail

across the indigo sea sky.
Everyone's on overreach:
if I double, will I die,
or have two lives instead of one,

longevity from being both
sexes according to wish?
The music is a seventies
glam-rock; a Bowie striptease:

is the singer on his knees
giving head a boy or girl?
The host looks like Duchamp in drag.
We're a transhuman species.

It comes naturally, this need;
at twelve I used my first lipstick;
glossed it to a red satin,
and something in me was freed

to state a claim, an independency,
like those of us who dress this way
waiting for the world to change,
the normal ones to go away.

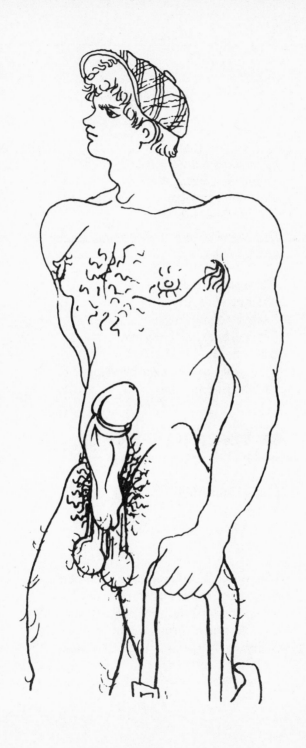

*Postcards*

(after Apollinaire)

### 1

Sacré Coeur the propitious stairs
Climb in a spiral We kiss
Conception makes way and pisses
It's like breathing tropical air
In a country full of spices

### 2

The dead of the rue St Vincent
Are not without balls
I saw a recent lay-in
Break from the family vault
And go screw Red Hot Lips
Who will raise you on her hips
Two steps from here

### 3

Rue d'Orchampt a song rang out
In the thick of a quarrel
A song
Rue d'Orchampt
Rang out
And I sang it to you delicious tart

### 4

Watch out Tourlaque here's the police
A gendarme menaces in the pissoir
Where a rent-boy with his balls in hock
On a poster of Jean Genet
Seems to fly towards the Orenoque

### 5

Joan the cow of Clichy
Shows her pachydermic ass
The turd she exhibits for us
Grins before standing out
As a comma on this stretch of whitewash

### 6

Marie-Antoinette

You fuck as an aperitif
It's better than Raphael
When a child of Brahmaputra
Sucks a cock at random then it's right
According to the *Kamasutra*

### 7

Her second skin black dress
Hardly conceals silk panties
And I dream of my cock's tight fit
in her ass-hole's cigar-cutter.

## Sensuality

Your tongue is sheathed in mauve satin,
one gold fingernail travels to exact
the way I reach a vertical axis
in expectation of your lips
finding me down there like a grape
rolled over to polish its sheen
before the black skin's lifted from the fruit
to show how sweet is the interior.

My teeth are softer than anemones,
releasing as they do your zip,
exposing a black bra-strap and the way
light hurries to study your spine
and stops at the divide above your hips,
as though I needed to enquire
about how a dress hangs in flower-folds
over the waist before it slips
to a buckled silk sculpture on the floor.

The things we do to each other,
they vitalize senses like biting lime
on a midsummer evening. Now you go
so quick you spin me like a top
working the heat into one vein,
and outside reassuringly I hear
as palliative to our heat, night rain.

## Leather

The guy's got ass, and the tight leather skin
reveals a liveability, creases
that hold to contour. And his fluency's
a provocation, translating movement

into suggestion. In this blue-hazed bar
they're panthers, sleek glossed jaguars, creatures
belonging to a scent, a pliancy
that's part a cult and part adaptable

to a rock-image ethos. Flick the zip,
and what jumps out has the intensity
of need as a direction – up and up
the loaded tip positioning for head.

The myth opens out as a certainty,
it's part of now and what is meaningful,
a unifying tie, fraternity
zigzagged by zips, going beyond the night

to where the action's pooled, the pleasure fast,
the outlaw hunted, excited to feel
a cool textured body in his embrace,
hands on his shoulders as he drops to kneel.

## Tomorrow's Twenty Million Stars Away

A silver chair faces a silver chair
across a square black floor. Two missile-shaped
exotic fish show on a screen,
piscine androids, their dart and flash
is like two tailing meteors.
A man floats right across the room
as though there is no gravity. He looks
for clues to someone else. The window-blind
when it's lifted discloses stars
so near, they're within easy reach. Blue, green,
approachable masses. The TV screen
depicts his counterpart. A woman floats
into coital position, unzips
a pink catsuit, it's a fluorescent skin.
She has no pubis, but an eye
opens in her navel. He focuses
his left eye on that point. She orgasms
from the directed beam. She disappears
into the back of things. The fish chase round
the lights in their aquarium,
and seem animated by what they've found.

## Schweppes

A place forgotten for its name.
He listened there to Bowie's 'Breaking Glass',
his doubtful boy-friend moodily
staring up outside the hotel,

the girl between them reading on the beach
in a narrow-thonged bikini.
Her eyes were turned inwards. She imagined
the future as a big black ball

she couldn't see around.
And was their carpet green or red,
their intimate things shared or separate,
the television screen on without sound?

He looked out at the surf-dazzle,
the white hotels around the bay.
The little things mattered more than the great.
Her silent speech was what they meant to say.

## Hook and Eye

Her hands go round on her suspender back,
working to part the black silk, separate
the halves; her stockings at her feet, sheer bunched
to slip over red toes. He watches her,
and it is often he performs this act
behind closed curtains with the storm outside
as big blue horses in a violet field,
the siesta dragging sails in his blood,
unlike this ritual of her lingerie,
the tricky hook-and-eye fastenings that snap
in stick-sharp cracklings before slipping free,
lazy or rapid as becomes the mood.

## *The Images*

She slips a strawberry in her mouth
and represents a scarlet lipstick line,
a perfect oval.
                    'What is there to do
about desire?' she says. 'The time you wait
fires poetry; a panther comes to meet
you, carrying a pink carnation in its mouth,
a woman you see from behind
runs naked into a green sea,
and coming out steps straight into your mind
and into satin sheets, a leopard curled
up on the floor opens a jasper eye,
then goes outside into the sun.
You need these things, the visionary
as it telescopes from the need.'

She walks from her dress and locks the door,
and tells me to anticipate the way
she purrs like a cat, and the images
are everywhere, are freed.

## Head

I crack her dress zip from behind; my friend
is seated on the other side, and she
lowers her breasts over his erection,
and holds off from his verticality.
And isn't this a Leonor Fini,
I hazard, we the men in drag, a red
hat on our model who has no eyebrows
and blue lips to state her androgyny.
We have a Warhol portrait on the wall;
Andy with cherokee hair facing out
at our far from discursive commentary.
Her lips lower for the fellatio
my friend's expecting; a blue lipstick mark
is a colour variation on red.
I have my way, and look round once to see
a black cat staring in through the window,
its two paws clapping for a champagne moth.
It's a slow process, this giving head.

## Kicks

I need the boost; the shift of dimension
that takes me someplace else: I'm on the move
through the rapid high of my momentum –
the mood shifting from disinterest to love

of quantifiable obsessions, speed
as it gets to me through fast music, light
as it directs colour, the scarlet dress
I've tacked to a black wall seems half in flight

from a pursuant, imaginary bull.
That old song 'Kicks' with its deviancy,
Lou Reed's psychosexual, drugged, mid-career
killer-role on 'Coney Island Baby'

returns me to a past in which I drank
for clarity, dressed as a transvestite,
a diamanté earring on my fly,
and looking for a poem walked the night

around the harbour precinct, blue on black,
a lonely ship's horn sounding in the bay.
I learnt to index madness, all the weird
losers who sponged their make-up in the day;

it was exhilaration, I would dare
almost anything – and the mood persists
to celebrate what is anomalous,
the studded bands I wear around my wrists,

the black G-string I strip to as a lift
to getting off; the music picks up beat
as I prepare to write, describing how
the cold objective vocals carry heat.

## Games

She appears naked: a leather cat-mask,
a black silk tie knotted round her wrists,

soft thigh-boots supple on the sprayed gold floor,
the camera open, picking up

on planes that touch its radius.
He sits dead centre in the room,

casual, diffident, inhaling a pink
carnation held in his leather-gloved hand,

swathed blond hair concealing his face,
his blue lipstick puckered to a cornflower.

The two might be rehearsing parts
for a gestured, erotic dénouement.

A second woman enters by another door
and flicks a bullwhip in the air,

she wears a cap and a rubber mini;
she looks like a new-age Marlon Brando.

A storm builds up outside: magenta clouds
mass to a packed crater, a tight

magnolia bud which will explode.
He continues to play indifference,

looking at neither while the two close in,
bathed red by a single spotlight.

## It Takes Two

It's making one geometry not two,
and Elaine works a bright globule of oil
over each nipple, finding points that Sue

expresses verbally. She's like a cat
in her abandonment, legs arched, thighs splayed,
and Elaine gets between, her body flat

as a guerrilla sniper. She can do
what to a man is the preliminary
more consummately, and she knows it's true

from the exchange of roles. They like it hot
and playful, tormenting only to please,
and one receives what the other has got,

alternately. It's a partnership,
and Elaine breaks open black, polished grapes,
retrieves one from the point of Sue's left hip,

before she's underneath and Sue's on top,
imparting friction. She breaks into flame.
She hopes those fingers and tongue never stop.

Later, they'll drink highballs. It is their life.
They have a Balthus, roses in a vase.
Sue is the husband and Elaine the wife.

## *Three*

You take me to a place I do not know;
your wife is there and valedictory
swans lift from water into air,

the migrants going and heard doing so.
I feel I've stepped from a book,
the cover a fictional door
into a different reality.
Your wife unzips her skirt
imaginatively for you, but real to me.
She pulls a violet envelope
out of a black stocking-top.
There are no words inside, just the imprint
of scarlet lips.
She places both my hands around her hips
and draws me in.
You sit alone, branched high into a tree
and whistle to the last paired swans,
two black, two white.
They carry roses to us in their beaks.

A pinkish mist comes down over red trees.
The three of us open a book
and lose ourselves inside. We reach
another place. Your husband kisses me.
We have our different modes of speech.

## G-spot

She places five stockinged toes in his hand
and five on his shoulder.
His fingers trace the nerve-routes that excite.
Their play's protracted; the delayed suspense
of opening a Chinese box.
Her trembling vibrates a glass stood
on the table. In an hour she'll reach
the perfect, sustained O,
a climactic vowel shaped like the moon.

It's darker outside. Inky blues
obscure the garden; the opposite house.
Both feet are cradled in his hand.
He orchestrates them with subtle tuning.
Her toenails type out a rhythmic pattern
through sheer black silk. Her storm will rock the bed
before he meets her with his own demand.

## Pink and Blue

He's pink, she's blue; they didn't understand
their fabled days, his friends,
her colleagues at a loss to know
how such incongruities match.
She brought him home red roses in the snow,
still crisply pleated from a cemetery.
He gave her a face-net she'd seen in *Vogue*;
their complementary warmth was weird.
They shared a satin bed with Art Deco
panels, but others guessed they kept
to their respective sides and slept.

She stole for him because it gave her kicks,
and undermined her role as an executive.
He made her leather toys and copied out
the poetry he loved. Auden's
valediction to the thirties
as 'a low, dishonest decade'.
Their life was unified by oddities;
he wore her lingerie, she his cologne.
He zipped her into leather when she went to raid

a polished row of limousines
for stereos. They married without sex.
He gave up making toys; she grew afraid.
She found help for her kleptomania.
He went off one day as he would have done,
leaving her red roses and the door-key
to a villa he'd inherited in the sun.

## *Tongue Dance*

A red flourish
as your lips open
to a carnation. Tongue
to tongue it's another
language, a peekaboo
creation, an anther
reversing to enter a flower.
Our rhythm expands
to other components,
a violent jazz, flamenco
dancers interlacing,
a probe that explores
the taste of the other's
arousal, seeds a rain forest
in the silk lining.
Little mauve antennae,
leaf-shaped concentration points
for the senses, inspired to beat quicker,
rhythmically, for what later
will lead to exploratory travel,
the entry wherever it will
be like a cave or a shell.

## Jewels
### (after Charles Baudelaire)

Abandoned, thighs splayed, yet her expertise
knew that the regalia of jewellery
offsetting her naked body would bring
the fetishist down on a single knee

to pore over the dazzling reflections
of stones rhythmically striking against gold;
a conflagration worked across the hips,
the body warm and oiled, the minerals cold.

Passive, obedient to my every touch,
couched high on cushions, but still out of reach
of possession, my longing for her grew
to the crisp fall of a wave on the beach.

Her eyes were a big cat's, tamed into trance,
and when she shifted she'd accentuate
each curve; already her audacity
had me anticipate the mounting spate . . .

Her long slim legs welcomed me like a vine,
her thighs undulating with beads of oil,
her nipples grown to black grapes, had me long
to feel the tightening of her cobra's coil.

Caught up by a spell I couldn't elude,
I broke from my crystal; dark and light
were the opposing forces, I advanced
towards abandon with the coming night.

Hinting at transvestism she combined
full hips with the thin torso of a boy.
Man or woman, it didn't matter which,
desire had fashioned a new sexual toy.

And with the lamp extinguished by her hand,
only blue firelight flickered in the room;
and every time my tongue formed a love-bite,
her skin reddened with an exotic bloom.

## Voyeur

About his hides he's secretive,
spots on his territorial map
are daily to be visited,
like someone returned to a trap,

sure that the steel has sprung a hare.
His stamping-ground is wooded heath,
his restive figure moves between
birch-trunks, or flat down, snakes beneath

bracken to gain a vantage-point
on the entangled geometry
of two engaged exclusively,
his and her hands exploratory

in ways he wishes were his own.
He visualizes sensation,
empathizing with both, alert
to each response, the slow motion

of hands tented beneath her skirt,
the rift in his divided fly,
where a red fingernail explores.
He lives each action with his eye,

and is on rare occasions chased,
flushed out of hiding, but is gone
through backwoods like a hunted fox,
finally left to run alone,

as stealth gains the ascendancy.
His need is greater than his fear,
both activate as stimuli
to bring him incautiously near,

to feed off two vicariously,
so caught up in their rhythmic dance,
he stands mesmerized, moon-struck, glazed,
like one dictated to by trance.

### *The Insatiable*
(after Charles Baudelaire)

Outrageous he-she, skin a cobalt dusk,
an obi's dream, a Faustian mirage,
perfume tinted with Havana and musk,
ebony body made for midnight's stage;

my need for you supersedes opium, wine,
a Nuits-Saint-Georges is nothing to your lips,
my sensual caravan moves like a vine
to ensnare the slow rhythm of your hips.

Your dark eyes are skylights into your mind,
my body's branded by your raging flame,
a Styxian sailor set out to find

the nine circular loops across the flood,
and burn in the underworld where you tame
tigers attracted to your boiling blood.

## Red Stains

### A Poetic History of Lipstick

*Red*
Three bright-red carp suspended as an aqueous haiku sit right beneath my reflection. It's like that, seeing the world upside-down, watching fish in the manner that images implode. Her lipstick stands out like two Matisse-red crescents. They are brought together as a carnation through which the tongue intrudes.

*Orange*
It's the shade the pilot wears when taking off. It's his cockpit ritual. That and the increased light inside his head. The skyline is heat-hazed. As he lifts into the sky he's obsessed by the idea of entering a parallel dimension. He'll land in a black, volcanic desert. The pyramid facing him will be a triangular arrangement of orange lips.

*Black*
The mime artist's mouth. The focal bruise of a Dietrich; the black tulip that was Billie Holiday's smile. A square, a locket, a corolla set in the face, an invitation to fellatio. In a black room he discovers himself. A woman walks out of the mirror and into his body. When he comes back to the world there's been an eclipse. Two men in black stand on a balcony making a salute to the sun.

*Pink*
Camellias are open in December. Lautrec got pink into almost everything. In Kandinsky the colour's an abstract volute. He remembers the black beret tilted towards her left eyebrow, the shocking-pink jacket finding its correlative in her lips. That winter she changed her name to Loraine. She left a wine-stain on the microphone. She migrated to a character in her song. She was double, getting away in the waiting car.

## Stranger to Stranger

Those many startled faces under stairs –
the boys of the seventies grown to men,
eclipsed by sexual fear. When will it end,
this risk of contagion? The protracted
shadow falling on leather, denim, ears
weighted with rings, silver crosses. Bad blood's
an invitation to meet death: black snake
sunning on every road. Field-fires,
shooting stars, a lover's bridge
over the impossibly flooded stream.
And who can get there, make it clear
through so many invitational nights?
It's harder now; the knit fraternity
fragments under pressure. These two engage
in caution, picking up in the city
and vulnerable – a stranger to stranger –
half resolved to go ahead, half slip free.

## Diana and Diana

That mean cat clones her lover. She's in song,
the royalties maintain perverse habits
in a penthouse. Doubles are doubles there,
two mirrors, two screens, two of everything
in a paired unity. They make up as halved
opposites; one side of the face blue-apricot,
the other mauve, the complement reversed.
They tune in to each other's thoughts. One sings,
the other copies without voice
in a stylized mime. They wear black leather
to offset bright emerald hair.
Diana and Diana. It's on-stage
the one excels, retrieves her buried past,
burning out, kicking up a cloud of dust
right on the valley's edge, a pebble gone,
a rain of clatter following.
She's learnt to translate it all into tone,
outrageous panache sustained at zero,
an ice-cool come-on from the microphone.
And it's intensity; the weird, the wild,
the madly incomparable.
The other keeps backstage. Love is stronger,
sex in the limousine that takes them back
to living high, dreaming of the next show.

## *The Sun*

(after Charles Baudelaire)

It's my stamping-ground. These old suburbs,
slatted Persian blinds hung at the windows
of yellowing houses; and half concealed,
a man slipping a woman's shoulder-straps
to catch her breasts. A heat wave rolls over
the city; fires the roofs as I search out
a chance rhyme in a corner, shadow-fence
with words that reveal a poem's figure
sketched out, burning its form into my nerves.

The reassuring sun lightens our blood;
opens the rose, has our anxiety
disperse; replenishes our dead brain-cells,
sees the hive stored with rich honey.

It's he who rejuvenates the crippled,
and marches in the new Gay Rights Parade;
and he who provides a fertility
to crops. How rich the harvest shows again.

And like a poet come down to cities,
he imparts beauty to the meanest things,
and like a king without his bodyguards,
he enters palaces, old warehouse yards.

## You'd Sleep with Anything
### (after Charles Baudelaire)

You skirt-hitched slut, you'd sleep with anyone
and anything. Boredom makes you perverse
and crave for kicks; you're up all night on drugs.
Your fetish is to bite a heart a day
and leave it bleeding in a used ashtray.
Your eyes light up like a jeweller's display,
or burn like fireworks at a festival,
but lack the moderation to assume
beauty must understate itself or lose.

You're nothing but a sex-machine. Your tricks
are vampirical on assorted pricks,
your shamelessness leaves you insensible
to how the mirror frames you as a tart.
But even you in your most private hours
must shrink from what's enacted on your bed,
the long, consummate nights of giving head
to clients, and the one mistake
that catches you My Leather Queen gives birth
incongruously to a child genius

who lives to duplicate your ways on earth.

## Purple Banana

Her finger trick creates a banana:
it is ophidian how he erects
and telescopes into her lipsticked pout
and undulates a slow motion
in and out, not a sixty-nine,
she crouched down on her haunches, bottom up
in air-sheer white panties.

She imagines a tongue teasing her crack
and he additional fingers on his balls,
they need inventives to participate
in sensory extravagance,
fluent conjunction of geometries,
two side by side, one flipped over,
the other on his back.

He eases his purple banana free
before it shoots its seeding galaxy.
Fellatio as an aperitif
stimulates the volcanic impetus
to other pleasures.

                She ascends a scale
of excruciating laughter;
it's guesswork what he does to her
and where he is, and over and over
their tensions twist round a molten core.

## Rubber

One girl wears a leather cap and net gloves,
the other a rubber skirt drawn so tight
it's a black skin. They're interlocked;
the net gloves interlace with hands
placed over studded breasts, and a tongue leads,
searching the ear's cavity, describing a line
the length of the curved spine
to a track over rubber, following
to the divide beneath a black G-string,
and finding a neat entry from behind.
They stay like that until they turn around,
one on the other, mutually working
towards an orgasm, that wave on wave
floods through their bodies. It is nothing new,
and in the aftermath the quiet rain
settles on rooftops. Lady sings the Blues.

## Nu Rose

### (painting by Matisse)

How centrally the blonde sustains the theme,
parting a yellow curtain on the day,
the light flooding her nudity
that's sensuous, and has she turned
an eye appraising her beauty?
the unseen figure tented by the sheets –
that section of the room's imaginary.

We know her as Lydia Delectorskaya;
black mouth, linear eyebrows, slanted eyes,
she has a ballet dancer's face.
The excess light dabbing at the window
behind her, with its aquamarine curtain
left open all night, has the subtle pink
that's toned into her skin. New light, new day;
and how the colours transmit energy –
the scarlet carpet, primary green palms,
the window's red and violet frame.

We wish that we could hear her speak
the thoughts expressed by her gesture;
some private erotic exchange,
before she busies herself with coffee,
finds a silk wrap and playfully
points a peach with her tongue, and calls his name.

## Our Time

We're living through it together, apart.
I tie imaginary scarlet ribbons
round your wrist
and link them to my heart.

And it's the odd catches me out, your bra
that's part black silk and part transparent mesh,
pointed to good effect; and how we keep
a sugar skull in a sweet-jar,
and a page open in the book
that's being written. And sometimes we play
Glen Gould's inventions playing Bach.

We're transient, so magnify our days
like autumn light standing beneath the trees
in an old apple orchard in Provence.
We're linked together so invisibly
each feels the other's impact on the thread.
I'm with you miles away, you me.
It's noon. You're naked in my head.

## *That Way*

The smell of warm black leather from your sleeve
gets me up high; hectic astringency
that leads me to pursue. Direct nerve-hit.
I want your mouth to open out in mine
like a double camellia,
a pink and white disclosing red and white
in the interior.

These nights I feel the anonymous crowd
reclaim me, faces met in sea-gardens,
a harbour's blankside wall.

And found because the impulse was that way,
the scarlet lip imprint on a white shirt,
the act of two the same, starlight
flecking the rhythm of a cobalt bay.
Either I or the other wouldn't stay.

My pen reclaims the risk; a close-up moon
cuts diamonds on the pane, as once under
a garden shelter looking out to sea
a locket jumped from a throat, the sky closed,
the bass notes throbbed with imminent thunder.

## Openly

They're two together. She and she.
Black lipstick, a gold-tipped black Sobranie,
and with the thin one gel has licked

a blown back wave, a Modigliani
narrowness of face, and they're in love
quite openly.
Here we stand gender on its head,
a café looking out to sea,
gay smooching, intruders pinned to the wall.

Marilyn and Jane.
They met and storm-kissed under summer rain,
and later loved impossibly, defiantly

all over town.
They share a red umbrella. Jane's black tie
will sometimes point a snake's head at the sky.

## Fellatio

Extempore or studied
the snake-charmer's fingers
lead to a flautist's

pressure on the tip.
A tulip's tight glower
before silking open

on a scarlet lip.
A protracted flicker
as though the tongue

untied a ribbon
slipped round the head.
A double friction,

both hand and mouth
work up from the base,
then alter the motion;

slow-coax and delay
the tingling summit,
enquire of each tremor's

vertical pointing.
The oval mouth spins,
makes a peppery hit.

The pauses are studied,
the cheetah rests on a low branch
while scaling the tree.

Later, the high spot,
the last before thunder,
equatorial, steamy, jungle-hot.

## House of Mirrors

.Today a note from the pornographer
and a copy of *Les onze milles verges.*
I have the house of mirrors to myself,
and climb enquiringly from shelf to shelf,
inviting curiosity.
A little red fish keeps me company

and opens a blue fan in a glass bowl.
A concealed lens monitors my movements,
he'll play it back on his return, the shots
of me in black stockings, black gloves,
or sitting legs arched on the bed,
painting my toenails red.

Mostly I invent fictions, characters,
I cross dress and become a man,
or watch myself on the toy rocking-horse.
I'm someone else for the long afternoon.

His letter is marked *Amsterdam.*
I think of eyebrow bridges, hurried clouds.
He'll return with the usual. Illicit,
explicitly sensational films. Not blue,

for that's the colour of the sky.
I run from mirror to mirror and act
my imaginative parts. I'll write a play

and run away, one
April day.

## Open Air
### (after Paul Éluard)

The shore with trembling hands
dropped down a staircase of mist
under the rain
You emerged quite naked
a pulsing false marble
coloured with morning
a treasure guarded by great beasts
who retained sunlight for you
beneath their wings
they were there without our seeing them

Beyond our night's walls
beyond our kisses' horizon
the hyena's contagious laughter
might well work at the dead bones
of beings who live one by one

We played at the sun at the rain at the sea
at only having one glance one sky and one sea –
ours.

## *Edge of Town*

Extensible, but never quite the same,
our meetings come to this, a place
of shadow, wasteland on the edge of town,
the sea behind us, a blue space
over the shoulder, nobody around
but those in sympathy.

                        I turn your face
full front, as though it were a first time discovered,
a secret opening out from the compact
to the impacting rose.
Lipstick on a man; we are two
outsiders under a wall,
talking of a future way,
tolerance – but in what century?
Blue-blue-blue-blue light surfs in from the bay.

## Girl Housebreaker

Cropped hair, a grizzled blonde, Marie
is so androgynously thin,
her body's a Giacometti pin,
her leather jacket's a rhino's
warped hide, her studded boots are hard
on the accelerator. Backing off
from contact, she's most often in a yard

tinkering, seeing to a store.
Her jacket logo's a death's head,
her uncompromisingly masculine
hand movements are too accented and laid
on a table reveal oil-stains, a red
paint-blotch. It's her undercover
movements indicate a psychology
that short changes, takes milk from a doorstep,
fruit from a stall, her jocular
pretence closing over something bitter,
alluring rind on lemon, lime.

A spate of obsessively mannered thefts,
only male items stolen, vandalized,
a wardrobe of suits aerosoled with paint,
one side only of the bed compromised,
was for its duration her singular
topic of conversation. Who?
Marie the loner, never blue
or emulative of her girl-friend's dates,
grew uncontactable, stormy,
took to breaking windows by day,
snatching handbags, contradicting the part
she played by night, her war on both sexes
considered as the work of two,
while she left town, madly painting a wall –

M on the arrow through a scarlet heart.

## Hers

Slow-motion alignment, her lips draw round
circles on her lover's areolas,
the intermeshing legs snaking to find
a grip, a centre in the hurricane,
black silk, worn denim, leather heaped
into a snake's discarded skin;
ten red carnations frostily pointing
towards the blue curtain.
Love that goes in and good and mediates
return to oneness, man the oddity
swinging his dipped liana, primal sun
rising to plummet back through the blind eye.

They're far from this: the way through's two the same,
late night, sensual threshing, complicity.
'We do it, and her husband never knows
that afterwards I paint her fingernails, her toes.'

### Bert

You've grown to be the permanence that life
denied us, deep-water statue
learning to achieve equilibrium
in all my contradictory moods –

you shift with how the current points.
Once sex was oral, a compensation
for how words wouldn't fit your mouth
but laboured to stammer
on a protracted oval vowel.

Dead, your fluency demands
I don't forget, translucent shine
of one who swam each day

winter and summer through in Half Moon Bay.
You are the drowned man in my head,
a deep-sea image, face drawn on the sand.

We have achieved different perspectives,
you've realized something I still don't know
in your release from time – how we get through
our shut dimensions if we really do
and deepen, existing to give
proof to the other that somewhere we live.

## At the Bottom

Where the stairs drop
to fidgety water,
you wait in a scow,
red lips, black beret,
hands knuckled with rings,
a book in your lap,
the pink tulips you've bought
showing fangs
in open throats. I trace
our clandestine meetings
back through the map of your face
to that first blue afternoon
in a bookshop, I browsing,
you pocketing Lautréamont's
detonative implosions,
striking by that an empathy,
so we met three streets away,
you thinking my pursuit
a store detective's, both of us
sharp with excitement,
out of breath, intuitively
making for the fluent green
light rising above a quay,
and taken unawares
you led me where I come today
stepping off the stairs.